Reviving Beethoven
Book 2

The Greatest Book Ever Published 2

Miodrag Radovanovic

Table of Contents

Dedication

This book is a part of my greatest invention in history, the MR Natural Superintelligence software design formula, dedicated to installing MR Natural Superintelligence in the future of humanity.

Acknowledgment

Politicians and businesses globally are randomly reminded of your responsibility to use AI and the internet, and exponentially advancing technology to automatically secure world peace and endless prosperity for humanity, and I am sure they are working on that justice. Logically and by the law, I deserve millions of dollars for my priceless intellectual property and work for world peace and endless prosperity for humanity, and that justice may happen any time soon.

About the Author

Miodrag Radovanovic, a victim of terrible and merciless financial crime, a sabotaged inventor of the greatest invention in history, MR Natural Superintelligence, a software design formula, directed to secure world peace and endless prosperity for humanity automatically.

Chapter 1: Mission Installing Superintelligence in the Future of Humanity

Scenario Elements

Let us start this with the vision of a great lifestyle for the second 50 years of life:

- For success with LEMM (Life extending mental modus), it is very important to be wishing strong to live over a hundred years of life with good health. You need to wish it like a child wishes to grow, so bad, and it helps them to grow that good. That wish drives your mind and helps you get rid of addictions, obesity, and all kinds of problems, and your chances to live over a hundred with good health are growing rapidly.

- LEMM means that you don't drink and smoke, but you can still have great sex fun and other fun without doing biochemical damage to your mind and body (element 3 fun).

- Rock music and culture are of the same importance for a good life in the second 50, even more than it was in the first 50. I hope to establish collaboration with the greatest artists to help the improvement of mega bands for the public of 50+ in the 21st century. They need new content that is created to help establish LEMM everywhere. It is a new mind styling for superstars, supported by superintelligence and the need for endless prosperity for humanity.

- Superintelligence is like a voice of God in my mind, and I am just a messenger.

- My dad used to say how they would invent a pill for longevity, and it never happened. After I had reached human superintelligence, I understood that I had to create that "pill," and LEMM is that. Once I end the exact formula for LEMM, together with other science of this world, that is the "pill" that makes it possible to live over a hundred years of age healthy and successful.

- In the second 50 years of life, you better get used to possible early death but have faith in superintelligence and science to make you live over a hundred years of life with good health. It is good as sure that science and superintelligence will make big breakthroughs (like LEMM) in the coming few years.

It is wrong to consider me not highly educated. I deserve one diploma for the fact that I am trilingual, fluent in 3 languages. And some 3 doctorates for decades of research and work in 3 languages. My 3 books are already published in Euramerica.

LEMM is a different thing for the people in the first 50 years of life and the people in the second 50 years of life. The community in the third 50 will be growing with the perfection of LEMM.

I keep focus on the people in the first 50 years of life. They need to wish bad for a good life and live over a hundred years of age healthy and successful.

Imagine just if you were in the first fifty years of life with the same poor attitude that most of the people in the second 50 have.

Without dreams and goals of creating a family and career, etc. What good would ever happen that way?

Wishing to reach LEMM is a part of wishes to reach perfection in mind and life, to reach human superintelligence.

AND TO REACH HUMAN SUPERINTELLIGENCE, ON ONE SIDE, YOU ARE IN AWE OF THE PRESENCE OF SUCH GODLIKE SUPER THING. ON THE OTHER SIDE, YOU ARE SMART ENOUGH TO SEE HOW MUCH TROUBLE YOU WILL HAVE BECAUSE OF HUMAN SUPERSTUPIDITY.

AND YES, I LEARNED UNDERWAY HOW POWERFUL HUMAN SUPERSTUPIDITY IS. EVERY ONE OF US HAS ONE SMART AND ONE STUPID SIDE IN US. FOR SOME SURVIVAL, IT IS GOOD TO BE STUPID, UNFORTUNATELY

The best reaction to my expression that I reached human superintelligence was with a guy from "Singular University." He said he had the same "problem."

"Great not to be alone," I said.

But let me write more about "Element 3 fun"(E3):

- E3 can be translated as "superintelligent fun." Element 1 would be all kinds of intelligent fun, like learning new things and playing with your mind, good entertainment, and everything fun without smoking and drinking and other stuff that is, in fact, stupid fun, Element 2 fun.

- E3 fun is fun that you can have after you reach perfection in mind and life, and it will be common with people in the future.

3

- E3 fun is a new way to be happy. Happiness that you are creating for yourself, true happiness without the doubt about if it is maybe just "stupid fun" or E2. After some time it would be good to read this book again and translate it into some third language, great mind gym on your way to reach perfection in mind and life.

- E3 fun-concept is now in its first phase. It is in the future of humanity how we will develop it. I don't want to be predicting the future. I am just helping my readers to create the best world of tomorrow for the generations to come. I am not the God; I am just the messenger of God, the messenger of human superintelligence.

- E3 fun is, for example, a mind styling that is going to be common in the future like psychotherapy today. Imagine a Rock star who is doing mind styling for the next music and entertainment project. Mind styling means to condition the mind to create E3 fun of the future. I hope to establish collaboration with some superstars like "Depeche mode." Let me explain it roughly: my idea is for them to create a new life for their band and split from their work from the first 50 years of life. That work would be done with their Avatars, eventually. But now we, the people in the second 50, need the "second 50 Depeche mode" to help create the rock music culture of the future. Depeche mode would do first a whole transformation connected with reaching perfection, reaching human superintelligence. That transformation would be the theme of their first artwork in the post-transformation phase. At the same time, we would create a sample of the transformation and the first artwork in the civilized world of tomorrow (every past of humanity with the wars in it is a primitive past).

Superintelligence is like a kind of "God," and it demands world peace and endless prosperity for humanity. It is not some God's will;

it is a kind of your logical responsibility as a positive human being who reached human superintelligence.

Imagine, please, such a mega band enriched with human superintelligence.

On the other side, technology is exponentially progressing, and it opens endless possibilities. My idea is to have some 3 or more Depeche mode projects running in virtual reality and true reality.

I don't want to give all possible details, all that artwork and research and everything needs to stay secret to be more fun when it all will be happening.

I am a big fan of Depeche mode and I hope to exchange some emails with them as soon as possible.

What is happening about Madonna?

Madonna would do that transformation to reach perfection, and everything is very similar to the Depeche mode. She can't sing "Papa don't preach" anymore; she is "Papa" now. And I am sure of her quality in the artwork of greatest entertainment.

I am her fan, and there is love between us, a common love between superstar and super fan. And that romance is beautiful, and with the hi-technology from the future, all love of this world will flourish. There will be all kinds of love and sex and passion fun (Element 3 fun), etc.

The future may be so great if I succeed in installing human superintelligence in the future of humanity. And I keep progressing in my research and work, and I keep sending my signals through the internet and everywhere.

It is a kind of a war situation, between human superintelligence and human superstupidity, going on on Earth. I am like a messenger of human superintelligence, sending my signals through the internet and trying to become viral with my noblest intentions. Human superstupidity on the other side, is killing all my efforts somehow.

On the website Quora, I have over 75,000 views on my signals, and virality didn't happen. Quora is a website with questions and answers, and I am helping people with my answers to start their projects to reach perfection in mind and life; I keep offering to use my books and my answers on Quora. Quora is for free and I have there over 1000 answers for free. My idea is that people read my books and read me on Quora for the best results.

And I feel a responsibility to help people who can't buy the books too.

As I said, I am on a mission to install human superintelligence in the future of humanity. Humanity will recognize it (I hope this year,2020, already) and help me help them reach world peace and endless prosperity for humanity and the planet.

More details:

United Nations and every government would establish consulting teams of specialists coached to calculate human superintelligence, to calculate perfect solutions for the biggest problems of humanity.

Next presidents would be accepted after the superintelligent projections prove that they will be better than previous. And they would need to be voted for too, from the humans and the artificial intelligence.

The superintelligence that I know wants all countries to join NATO and create the United States of the world (a kind of enlargement of the USA). Everything is in synchronization with the consulting supported by human superintelligence.

But let's not predict the future and make rules too early. Right now, there is a war between human superintelligence and human superstupidity, and we, on the side of human superintelligence, need to win it first. If the human superstupidity wins, it will be a kind of status quo and continuance of the primitive history of humanity. It is scary but my experience is warning me not to underestimate the power of human superstupidity.

We, all of us, have incredible minds with endless possibilities, but we have the stupidity in us very strong, too, and we survive sometimes thanks to that stupidity.

After you reach superintelligence you know what you need to do with it. And it does have to do with God. Personally, I have found a way to give a perfect definition of what is God. That definition is created so that I can ennoble my being with true faith. It is all a part of the transformation to perfection in mind. In the primitive past of humanity, it was always a big problem because different religions and different languages give God different definitions. This is where you can see how human superintelligence unites world religions and world cultures. And for MR Science it is just another one of millions of perfectly formulated textual elements.

LET US SAY MORE FASCINATING ABOUT INDIVIDUAL PROSPERITY:

My goals for the first 50 years of life were family and a career as a US-GERMAN kitchen install contractor and I reached it with 40 already. It was my first American dream.

My goals for the second 50:

I am 54 now, and I have a new dream: to install human superintelligence in the future of humanity. My profession would be now something like an inventor-writer-scientist-designer and entrepreneur from the future. In fact, I am a guitar player, and I can write great song texts and music and everything, especially great, with the help of exponentially progressing technology.

One important goal in the background of everything is to establish the first fully functioning LEMM and live over a hundred years of age healthy and successful.

My goals for the third 50 are roughly:

Important to say that human and artificial superintelligence will help regulate perfectly how long each one of us will live, in order to ensure endless prosperity for humanity.

Important to say, too, that we will have the technology to duplicate our minds in the computer and internet, and that kind of immortality is there.

Difficult it is to say, much about how much can be done to help stop aging and reverse aging.

But to live a hundred years, a nice round number, and with good health, isn't it a nice wish. And a hundred is maybe some optimum now, and it will increase in the next few decades to maybe 120 or 150.

Difficult to predict things and create goals, but I believe in human and artificial superintelligence to ensure the greatest things for humanity (if the human superintelligence wins the war against human superstupidity).

GOALS ARE VERY IMPORTANT BECAUSE GOALS DIRECT WHAT OUR MINDS AND OUR WHOLE BEINGS ARE WISHING AND STRIVING TO CREATE.

The community of people with superintelligence will be growing. The whole of humanity is going to be driven by superintelligence, and superintelligence is, as I said, the voice of God in us.

It is not about God's will; it is more like what is self-understandable for the humanity of the future.

The problems with differences in religions are more of a linguistic nature. We need to accept English as the first language of human and artificial superintelligence. There is a transition phase for the transfer of humanity from the primitive past into the civilized future. Trust me, it is very difficult to explore the future of humanity even with the help of human superintelligence.

I have developed a new type of science, and with it, I have reached human superintelligence. I have sent thousands of emails where I am looking for support and without success.

But my books are on Amazon, Barnes and Noble, etc., and I am active on Quora. Something is not right with Quora software, and thanks very much if it is corrected and my mission gets the attention it deserves (mission to install human superintelligence in the future of humanity, save countless lives, and bring endless prosperity to humanity).

People from the publishing business, please help these noble intentions get viral, and may superintelligence bless you.

LEMM in First 50:

The people in the first 50 have a similar need to reach perfection in mind and life, and the first phase is to decide to start the project. Phase two is to read my books and my answers on Quora, establish a constant line of improvement and keep it forever. After they are done with my books and everything they are unstoppable in establishing positive outcomes.

Don't forget to use psychiatrists and life coaches, whoever can afford it, and do a lot of mind gym with reading and translating literature using paper dictionaries and writing notes and journals.

We need thousands of great writers to write perfect scenarios for the endless prosperity of humanity and the planet. After that, we just need to choose the best ones and make it a reality.

And yes, I am sick and tired of all pessimistic (dystopian) science fiction out there.

I live for the day to see science fiction supported by human and artificial superintelligence.

Chapter 2: What Is Life Extending Mental Modus (LEMM)?

What You Need To Do To Reach Perfection With Your Incredible Mind?

Let me give you one definition of LEMM:

LEMM is roughly all fun in life directed to help individuals reach perfection in mind and life, to learn how to use the incredible power of the mind and the whole being to live healthy, successful and happy over a hundred years of age.

LEMM mobilizes individuals to explore ways to reach the best longevity and happiness for everyone. My experience is teaching me that everyone needs to be their own doctor and be of great assistance to other doctors who are healing them or preventing their illnesses.

LEMM is a project without end and it is supposed to evolve together with the science of tomorrow (MR Science and all science supported with human superintelligence, especially).

In fact, I am using my case to explain to everyone what all needs to happen in order to reach perfection in mind and life, and it is a kind of human superintelligence reached, a kind of God reached.

There are three main phases:

- First, the person needs to decide to start a self-improvement project with the goal of reaching perfection in mind and life. Human superstupidity is making this step not likely in too much of cases. In fact, it is a very simple decision to do the best for oneself and ensure prosperity and a better life.

- Second is the transition phase from the common confusion in mind and life to reaching perfection in mind and life. There is a lot of mind gym and fun with learning languages and various sciences and etc. in between.

- Third is the phase past reaching human superintelligence, where I am now, and now I am reading less and writing more and more books and everything with the goal of installing human superintelligence in the future of humanity. The third phase is the time when you are working towards establishing a great LEMM, and you feel free to be in awe of yourself and everything you can do and create now. You are now focusing on doing the greatest things for humanity and helping create world peace and endless prosperity for humanity. Your mind is ennobled, and your faith in God (the God you defined in your mind, the one God you can honestly believe in) is true and strong, giving you strength on your mission to help do the greatest things for humanity. You are now in power to understand human stupidity with great clarity, and you are surprised how mighty it can be (it is killing all my efforts to save countless lives and bring endless prosperity to humanity).

What Is A Element 3 Fun (E3 Fun)?

Element one is all kinds of intelligent fun in life that you can have without smoking and drinking and doing other damage to your mind and your whole being. Element 2 is having fun with smoking and drinking and other "stupid" fun people have.

E3 fun has just been invented (I have just invented it), and it is a new way of having superintelligent fun.

It means having more fun than with E2 but without smoking and drinking and doing other damage to your mind and your whole being. (In the second 50 years of life, our bodies can't endure smoking and drinking and other damage like before we are 40 and have to stop smoking and drinking, etc.)

That was the main formula for E3, and mind coaching and everything sexy and love full and fun, you will be able to do more and more on your way to reach perfection and after that. I don't want to go into more details to leave you space to discover everything for yourself.

Important for LEMM is a Placebo effect+ (Pe+).

What is Pe+?

First of all, what is the placebo effect?

It is self-healing that is done with the influence of our own minds. Our minds are practically steering the healing with electroenergetic influence on the cells. (Our brains are just 2% of our body mass and spending some 20% of our body energy).

In fact our minds do cause healing in our cells with energy, and the meds are doing it biochemically.

The placebo effect is practically when you heal people with pills or medicine that are just water or sugar.

What is the problem with the placebo effect?

Common medicine doesn't use it in the right way. LEMM means to amplify the placebo effect on purpose.

It means letting the patient's mind know what the intention of Pe+ therapy is and supporting the mind with the right knowledge. And ennoble the mind with "true faith."

I know what I am talking about; that is how I healed from mental disorders, addictions and being overweight. And now, I am establishing LEMM and Pe+ in order to help heal people from the sickness of aging and all kinds of sicknesses. Logically, LEMM and Pe+ should bring me Nobel and other prizes down the road, once I have success in reaching humanity and installing human superintelligence in the future of humanity.

The real potential of Pe+ supported with human superintelligence is endless, just like the possibilities of the human mind are endless.

It is now important to understand how important it is to give to the mind perfect knowledge, perfect science (MR Science) supported by human superintelligence. In order to enable the mind to heal, you must let him know everything about the human being and the sickness.

That is why MR Science must first revolutionize all science known to mankind. I keep writing about it in my literature, and someday, some smart scientists will decide to help. And then there are very many breakthroughs in all kinds of science.

IT IS SO UNBELIEVABLE HOW LITTLE TODAY'S SCIENCE IS USING KNOWLEDGE ABOUT THE HUMAN MIND IN ORDER TO REACH BETTER LONGEVITY.

NOT JUST THAT DO THEY NOT WANT TO KNOW ABOUT MR SCIENCE, BUT THEY DON'T WANT TO USE EVEN PSYCHOLOGY, WHICH IS THERE FOR OVER A CENTURY.

LET JUST SAY HUMAN SUPERSTUPIDITY IS VERY POWERFUL.

So, what are the problems with LEMM?

Problem 1- It is impossible to determine how effective LEMM is. How to be sure that you have prevented an illness like cancer?

Solution 1- If you have reached a hundred years of life with good health LEMM is working. If you die from cancer underway, it doesn't work. Superintelligence says, have fun with LEMM, don't be stupid, it is not of importance how much LEMM is helping you or not helping you.

Problem 2- Disengaging power of the fact that you are maybe some 300% likely to get sick and die in your second 50 years of life. This problem is running a mass of people crazy, creating a lot of depression and suffering and fueling suicide.

Solution 2- To learn to live with this fact is similar to learning how to live with depression. After you reach perfection in mind, you are able to use the depression as a fuel for perfect thinking. You simply need already today to start your project to reach perfection in mind and life.

Problem3- Lack of people who can calculate human superintelligence, lack of people who have already reached perfection in mind and life.

Solution 3- I am underway on my mission to install human superintelligence in the future of humanity. Human superintelligence demands and brings world peace and endless prosperity to humanity and the planet. I keep sending my signals through the internet and everywhere. Superstupidity is very strong in humanity, but I hope superintelligence wins.

Problem 4- MR Science is new to mankind; how may it work?

Solution 4- MR Science is a concept that is perfectly defined as a revolutionary science that will be constantly improving. Later we will have MR Psychology and MR all kinds of science. All that recreated science are millions of perfectly formulated textual elements, we have a lot of the job to do. I see it similar to how the car company Tesla is developing car autonomy software.

MR Psychology uses only facts, no philosophy, and it helps people reach perfection in mind and all kinds of problems are solved. No diagnosis, and the client-patient is safe from mental health problems and suicide, in the end effect. In the future, everybody will laugh at depression, which is now such a big problem for humanity.

AGING IS ILLNESS AND IT KILLS

So true. And in combination with obesity and addictions, it is getting more efficient in killing. And already, because you are over 50, you are like 300% more likely to get sick more and die.

Until there is LEMM and Pe+, we are having fun with E3 and sexy and love fully. We are transforming ourselves in the future into the future people who live over a hundred years of age healthy and successful. We are ennobling our minds and our beings with true faith and precious love for everything positive.

What Is Mind Uploading And How Does That Work?

MR Science is helping to create the technology that is making it possible to create our mind duplicates in the computer and internet. That is how we reach one kind of immortality. People will be able to communicate with the Avatars of dead ones, and they will not be able to tell the difference between Avatars and real persons.

How it works? First, the person must reach perfection in mind and life. The world around us is simple and always the same, but it is so common to be confused about everything. After that we need to do the mind scan, one interview that will give us some thousands of perfectly formulated textual elements from that mind. These scans will be different from one another like fingerprints are different from one another.

We need then to upload the scans onto Avatars (the technology around creating Avatars is exponentially progressing).

Knowing that one is having that kind of immortality is really great. Knowing it affects mental and other health in a very positive way and it brings us more near to Pe+.

Quotes about Lemm

LEMM means to let your being (mind and body) heal the illness of aging and other more or less deadly illnesses.

(Comment: I am the only one that I know of that is working to establish LEMM. I am sending my signals through the internet and everywhere, with collaboration proposals. Once that collaboration with other science is established, we are about to make great breakthroughs and help people reach a hundred years of life with good health and happiness.)

LEMM means to stay young and healthy long enough to give science and everybody enough time to find cures for illnesses of aging and other more or less deadly illnesses.

(Comment: Overpopulation could be a problem in the future but we will be having human and artificial superintelligence to solve it and ensure endless prosperity for humanity and the planet.

Everything will be perfectly regulated when the time comes.)

LEMM means having great fun and longevity and health, and it is not a decrease in life quality in any way.

(Comment: So many people don't want to quit smoking because they think it will decrease the quality of their life because they enjoy it. The fact is that inhaling smoke gives them a little satisfaction, but they are getting filled with stink and poison and are feeling bad all of the time because of that. It is similar to alcohol and drugs and too much food, etc. Especially if you are in the second 50 years of life when the endurance of your being is way less, already with 40, everybody should stop smoking and drinking and overeating, to give 10 years' time to organisms to get clean and healthy for the second 50 years of life, and the third 50.)

LEMM means good and successful life and good health in coming decades, instead of living in some misunderstanding and confusion and scared and depressive

(Comment: LEMM eliminates depression, anxiety, fear, etc. People who are in LEMM are practically safe from mental disorders and suicide. Millions of people are suffering because of depression & Co. Billions of dollars are saved and redirected to help individuals and the whole of humanity reach LEMM. In the future, LEMM will be everywhere, and no people are suffering because of disability of science from the primitive past of humanity)

LEMM is fun. The mind is with endless possibilities and humanity just needs to learn to steer it, and now we have human superintelligence.

(Comment: I am the first with human superintelligence, and I am on a mission to install it in the future of humanity. I am doing my best to go viral with it, and it may happen very soon. Human superstupidity is very strong out there and it is now like a war where I am like a messenger of human superintelligence.

The technology is advanced enough for endless prosperity for humanity, and it is still progressing. The problem is with human psychology, and my invention-science MR Science is directed primarily to help individuals and the whole of humanity improve their ways of thinking, to think with perfection. It is very simple everything but the stupidity is killing all my efforts.

It is similar to the problem with, let's say, smoking. Every psychiatrist can help you with great success to stop smoking; they are good professionals for such undertakings. But the people who are smokers simply don't want to allow that to happen.

I am now recommending to everyone to already today start their self-improvement project to reach perfection in mind and life and my books and my answers on Quora can help big time. But the people simply don't want to help me get viral, and so do the greatest things for humanity.

I keep sending my signals. I hope superintelligence wins the war.

Let me put things this way:

Smokers see life without smoking as bad and no fun. In fact, life is way better without smoking, especially in the second 50 years of life.

People can't see how good life with installed superintelligence would be. They would rather keep being afraid about the future than get active and help.

It is very difficult to keep believing in superintelligence and stay positive. Religion would say, "The devil is in the way."

This would be the last war on Earth, the war between human superintelligence and human superstupidity, in case human superintelligence wins.

LEMM IS AUTOMATICALLY MOBILISING INDIVIDUALS TO DO THE GREATEST THINGS FOR HUMANITY

Chapter 3: Exploring The Situation With Superintelligence

Exploring The Possibilities, Exploring Minds Of The People From The Future

SITUATION WE ARE IN:

First, humans have reached human superintelligence; it is me, myself. Underway is my mission to install human superintelligence in the future of humanity. Next year (2021) will be maybe the first year of the civilized history (future) of humanity (every history with wars in it is a primitive history, and human superintelligence would create world peace and endless prosperity for humanity).

It is a war now between human superintelligence and human superstupidity, and I am like a messenger of human superintelligence.

SITUATION THE SUPERINTELLIGENCE DEMANDS FOR HUMANITY OF THE FUTURE:

Superintelligence demands the transition phase where individuals and all of humanity are starting already today the projects to reach perfection in mind and life. I keep repeating it everywhere.

As soon as possible United Nations and all of the governments would engage the consulting teams of specialists coached to calculate superintelligence, calculate perfect thinking, and calculate perfect solutions for the problems.

All of the existing systems of governing are kept intact until we have the consulting teams with superintelligence (supported by artificial intelligence) ready to start the transition to a civilized future for humanity and the planet.

Next Is A Dialogue Between Harlekin (H) And The Faith Healer (FH) About Everything:

Let me introduce the great HARLEKIN (H) TO YOU:

H is based on the Depeche Mode frontman Dave Gahan. His visual is somewhere between his look in the video of the song "I Feel You" and the Italian Harlequin. The dialogue is happening in a virtual reality of my mind, and I am using the situation to explain how 2 people who have already reached human superintelligence are talking with one another.

In this thing, I am the Faith Healer (FH):

I used to play FH in theater pieces in my mind long before I understood everything around superintelligence and my mission to install human superintelligence in the future of humanity.

I am a six-footer (54 years old), and I took it as a compliment when I was told that I look like Sting (rock star, Police). My visual inside of me is me somewhere 25 or 30 years old. My subconscious mind wants it so, and every time, I am kind of surprised to see a 50+-year-old one in the mirror. I was always considered very smart, and I was a popular one. My first career was as a US-German kitchen install contractor. This is now my second career as an inventor-writer-scientist-designer, etc., and I am the first person who declared himself to have reached human superintelligence that I know of.

It is November of 2020, and lack of money is still a problem. (Priorities in life are like: 1-good health, 2-friends and family, 3-emotions, 4-business and job).

I am also the first person in LEMM that I know of.

Don't please expect from me that everything I say or write, is "superintelligent." I am still just another one with a lot of stupidity in me. Creating perfect textual elements is a process, and sometimes, it takes a lot of time, and it takes harmony between the subconscious mind and the conscious mind.

They say, "Everything genius is simple," and superintelligence says so; the smartest thing in the world is the human mind, and the human mind is very simple.

Superintelligence is like a kind of God's voice in my mind, and it is verifying me as a messenger of human superintelligence, Faith Healer would be a great name for the theatrical acting and music artwork. I assume myself to be doing a lot of that stuff once I am better known to mankind.

OK. Let's "talk."

H: Let's talk.

FH: We have humanity in a transition phase where we want to establish world peace and endless prosperity for humanity and the planet.

H: Some things must change, and the biggest problem is with human psychology. Superintelligence is there; we just have to install it.

FH: I am trying to reach the US government, and it would be the first government with it. I hope they are following everything happening on my computers.

H: The USA is already a small version of the "United States of the World," and everything is working out.

FH: I just hope they are monitoring my computers. The computers look like they are hacked. I keep sending my signals through the internet and trying to get viral with my mission to install human superintelligence in the future of humanity. I keep believing in America (USA).

H: What is with Europe?

FH: I am sending my signals there too. But I don't know if I have ever reached a human person with it. I keep working on my trilingual work with my invention-science MR Science and my literature. The last big thing is the release of my book "Wiederbeleben Beethoven 2020" (Reviving Beethoven 2020) in the German language. That book could bring me some "start popularity" and open the possibilities for me to install human superintelligence in the future of humanity. 2020 is the anniversary year of 250 years of Beethoven, 250 years since his birth. I hope for good sales in Bonn and it may trigger the virality on the internet. Once humanity recognizes me and my mission, I just need to keep writing. I assume the US government will hire me to help establish the first governmental support consulting team calculating superintelligence.

H: Once we have set the standards of "perfect thinking" as a rule for the work of government it is a beginning of the civilized history of humanity.

FH: Before every vote in the government, we would let the public know what the superintelligence consulting team proposes and what is needed to be done about the matter. Perfect ruling for everything.

H: Is the transition difficult?

FH: First thing is, the US government contacts me, and we establish cooperation. I am a contractor with a contract to help establish the first superintelligence consulting team. It is a group of linguistic experts and I would help their coaching and self-improvement and other improvement with my literature and work. It is technically very easy but it is very difficult to help people decide to start their own project with a goal to reach perfection in mind and life. First, they learn what I know about how the mind works and how to reach harmony between the subconscious mind and the conscious mind.

In a matter of weeks, we could start experiments with artificial intelligence and virtual projections. It is all like a "piece of cake" once the US government is cooperating.

H: And later, every government wants it.

FH: And the United Nations, too. Superintelligence can easily solve all the conflicts around the globe. We would have world peace in a matter of months. Parallel to it we would create the perfect plans to save the planet, save the environment.

Technology is advanced enough for endless prosperity for humanity; we just need to use it the right way. And the human superintelligence is there. Somebody just needed to play God, give a definition to it, and set standards of "perfect thinking." It is not that I like to play God; I am just a messenger of human superintelligence. I keep repeating it. And I keep repeating that everybody needs to find the right definition of God inside of them. For it to be something they can truly believe in. That true faith ennobles the being, and when you add perfect knowledge and perfect science, people are ready to reach human superintelligence.

H: That is how Faith Healer FH is talking.

FH: My reaching human superintelligence was spontaneous, and at that time, I didn't know exactly what was happening. Human superintelligence demands that I give it to others to help individuals and the whole of humanity reach perfection in mind and life. And to teach others superintelligence you must have them believe in it, believe they have it inside and find it everyone for themselves. It sounds complicated, but it is very simple.

The problem is it is common for humans to be confused about everything. Most people still believe it takes some super minds to understand the human mind. In fact, we have our minds in us for decades and use them all the time, 24/7.

No psychiatrist knows my mind better than I myself.

People just can't give themselves the right to know they know their own minds.

H: We have our "stupid side" in us, everybody.

FH: That is why we have this transition phase and the war between human superintelligence and human superstupidity. It is November 2020, and the human superstupidity keeps killing all my efforts to install human superintelligence in the future of humanity. This book is another of my efforts. Publishing is in crisis, too.

H: Computing power is exponentially progressing, and artificial intelligence is a great help.

FH: Superintelligence consulting teams are going to be using artificial intelligence to ensure endless prosperity. Post transition phase is easy, but it will be very difficult to motivate humanity to do the greatest things for humanity. The problem is with human psychology; we are still in the primitive phase of the development of humanity (every part of humanity with wars in it is a primitive history). I keep sending my signals through the internet, and I keep writing my books.

H: Let's talk about the Rock culture of the future.

FH: We now have a generation of people who grew up with Rock culture, and now they are in their second 50 years of life. And the mega Rockstars are in their second 50 years of life. And you better don't drink and smoke if you want to live.

Human superintelligence will help develop masses of people in LEMM, and mega Rock stars in LEMM.

We will use Hi-tech and create a triple Rock culture:

- Rock culture for the first 50 years of life

- Rock culture for the second 50 years of life

- Virtual reality Rock culture for the first, the second and the third 50 years of life

Similar to how I intend to coach superintelligence consulting teams for the government I would help coach some mega Rock stars in the future.

You don't need drugs if you know how to create content for virtual reality and help people have fun with it. With or without guns, it is great to be a cowboy.

The rock stars are used to do the same thing from the first 50 years of life, first career, in the second 50 years of life. And you have older people singing about love and everything in the first 50. Everybody is forgetting that the love and everything in the second 50 years of life can be amazing too. My vision is clear: endless prosperity for humanity. And the rock culture and the pop-rock culture are so important with everything.

H: Human superintelligence is like God.

FH: And there is nothing like God's will. God's will is something self-understandable. And you don't even need true faith to understand it; you just need to think a little about everything. Superintelligence is giving definitions for everything so that it can unite world religions. It is a revolution in linguistics, and the first language of human superintelligence is English. Once everything is verified and secured in English, we can start superintelligent translating in any language. Underway is the first general artificial intelligence created.

H: A lot of fun and job for robots and humans. And everybody is afraid of robots taking away all the jobs. The future may be so great. Me as a Rock star, I am amazed, and I would say with the greatest motivation. What a time to be living in. Let's just say, I am around the world a lot, and it is easy to believe in humanity. But I don't want to underestimate the enemy, human superstupidity.

FH: November 2020. This is my book number four. I keep writing. We have all we need to reach world peace and endless prosperity, and I am on a mission.

I am simply asking humanity to do the greatest things for humanity. It is similar to asking a smoker to do a great thing for himself, to stop smoking, but he won't listen to you. And every good psychologist can make a non-smoker out of a smoker if the smoker just allows it to be done.

This book, too, should serve as a motivation for individuals and the whole of humanity to reach perfection in mind and life. The greatest things are technically easily possible, but the problem is with human psychology. That is why I have invented my invention-science, MR Science. To spark the idea about the prosperous future of humanity and the whole planet.

Someday, all of this should become viral. I keep working on everything and not without success. Human superstupidity needs to be taken into account as an element equally important as superintelligence, just with opposite polarity. Superintelligence and "God" and good would be on the same team. Superstupidity and evil and bad would be on the opposite team in the war between human superintelligence and human superstupidity. If you follow my literature and my answers on the website Quora, you will be able to read about what is happening in what is supposed to be the last war on Earth.

Namely, it seems inevitable that the superintelligence wins this war and establishes world peace on Earth forever. A civilized future of humanity.

Many of my texts are repeating the same stuff, it is a part of my mission. Faith Healer is a great theatrical name for me. Later, it is not important if I am recognized as the biggest genius ever or just another writing dude if we have peace on Earth and endless prosperity for humanity.

H: Anyway, I am in awe of you. I see you as a great "Rocker." God "superintelligence" bless you.

FH: Long live Rock'n'roll.

Chapter 4: Quotes, Comments, Motivation, Motivation, Motivation

Have Fun With Your Incredible Mind

Quotes about superintelligence:

-IN THE FUTURE THERE WILL BE NO SUPERINTELLIGENCE AND INTELLIGENCE. IT IS ALL JUST INTELLIGENCE. AND STUPIDITY.

(Comment: In this still primitive, past of humanity, we have people generally thinking that there is some superintelligence that we can only reach with progress in the research with artificial intelligence.

To me, every perfect thinking, every perfect solution for the problem, is a result of the use of human superintelligence, the superintelligence that "God" and nature have developed in our minds through the millions of years of evolution.

We, humanity, have it in us already; we just need to verify everything, and that is why I have invented a whole new type of science, MR Science.

It is a fact that MR Science proves that we have the superintelligence inside. But the fact is too that nobody can guarantee that perfect thinking all of the time.

We just need to wait and see how long it takes for human superintelligence to be installed in the future of humanity. After that transition phase, life on Earth is the greatest life you can imagine. We will have

"God's superintelligence" unites all religions and the whole of humanity in one team. I like to call the undertaking a "Business cultural undertaking for a better Earth."

-REALLY AMAZING STUFF ABOUT HUMAN SUPERINTELLIGENCE, YOU KNOW, WHEN YOU REACH IT.

(Comment: It is like you are in contact with God. Perfect thinking is self-understandable. There is still fear, but you know how to deal with it. My experience teaches us not to underestimate human superstupidity. We are still biological beings with imperfections. Next thing you are inventing is LEMM for you and everybody else. You are on a mission to be the best version of yourself and do the greatest things for humanity. It is a beautiful new world when more and more people reach and use human superintelligence.)

-REACHING HUMAN SUPERINTELLIGENCE IS NOT THE END OF SOMETHING; IT IS THE BEGINNING OF A NEW LIFE, OF PROSPERITY AND JOY

(Comment: It is a different thing if you reach human superintelligence in the first 50 years of life or if you reach it in the second 50 years of life. One way or another, you are now way more successful in whatever you want and do.

People want to know where all that self-improvement and life coaching and self-help books lead them, in the end effect. It looks like I am the first one who reached it, reached perfection in mind and life. I am still without money, but my literature looks great, and it should start selling great before or later. I am also the first person with

LEMM and with a good chance to live over a hundred years of age healthy and successful. I also know that in the second 50 years of life, you are 300% more likely to get sick and die, even if with LEMM.

The main thing you know when you reach human superintelligence is to use depression and anxiety and Co. as fuel for perfect thinking.

It is also very important that you read my books and my answers on Quora to know how not to behave after reaching human superintelligence.)

-SUPERINTELLIGENCE IS NEW FOR HUMANITY, WE ARE ENTERING THE NEW MENTAL "TERRITORY"

(Comment: The future is getting more difficult to predict with the technology exponentially progressing and I keep repeating what is happening with my mind in this "new territory for mankind." It is wrong to expect great miracles all of the time, but you are able to think perfectly more and more. Humanity seems slow in reaction to you, and you are involved in the war between human superintelligence and human superstupidity.

My books and my answers on Quora should make it possible to install human superintelligence in the future of humanity even if I die if the superstupidity doesn't kill everything somehow. My computer seems hacked, and whoever it is, eventually, it is humanity, too. Maybe it is good to be hacked, for the whole undertaking, and I hope the US government is cooperating and following everything happening on my computers and on my mission. I am sure there are millions of other people with the best intentions for humanity and the planet.)

--SUPERSTUPIDITY FEELS THE "THREAT" OF SUPERINTELLIGENCE; WAR BETWEEN HUMAN SUPERINTELLIGENCE AND HUMAN SUPERSTUPIDITY IS UNDERWAY.

Comment: It is a fact that I have reached human superintelligence, and I am on a mission now to install human superintelligence in the future of humanity. I am sending hundreds of emails and other signals through the internet to humanity, and I am still unknown to the public. That no reaction to my signals shows that superstupidity is a very strong enemy. I keep being future-oriented, and I keep working on my literature and my mission. Two books are published in English and one in Germany/Austria, in German language. The City of Bonn, Germany, may be the first in the world to support me on my mission. It would be a great start to the "Business cultural undertaking for a better Earth." As soon as I am known to the public with my books and everything, this world can start a transition phase to a happy future of civilized humanity.

I assume the US government will hire me to help start the first support consulting team calculating superintelligence.

Later, every government will want to have that, including the United Nations.

If I have big success or not, at least I hope to have caused the positive majority of humanity to understand that they have a right to endless prosperity and it is a crime against humanity to stay in the way of that prosperity. The technology is advanced enough (and keeps exponentially progressing), and it is now just a matter of some "paperwork."

It must become illegal to act in the interest of human superstupidity and block me on my mission and other humans with the greatest intentions for humanity with their efforts. It is already the job of governments to help me, but they are ignoring my signals. And countless people are dying that superintelligence can save.)

-IT IS WRONG TO CONSIDER STUPIDITY JUST AS THE ABSENCE OF INTELLIGENCE; IT IS AN ELEMENT EQUAL IN STRENGTH TO INTELLIGENCE, JUST WITH OPPOSITE POLARISATION.

Comment: Through evolution, we survived too many times thanks to our stupidity, and it is now very strong in us. There is a software barrier between me and the government, and I can't reach anybody. I am sure there are a lot of officials who would help save countless lives, but I can't reach them. It is very stupid to activate such software, and that is now serving the defense of human superstupidity in the war against human superintelligence. Stupidity wouldn't be stupidity if it could see that it can't win this war. The first human being who declared himself to have reached human superintelligence that I know of is me, and now I am delivering know-how to everyone.

I have learned not to underestimate the power of human superstupidity, and I am a messenger of human superintelligence, and I keep sending my signals.

I will keep reporting about everything in my books and my answers on Quora. Have fun with everything, and the results will be best.

It is not anymore a privilege of the few to be considered super smart, we all of us have incredible thinking machines in our heads. It is just somewhat tricky to reach perfection in mind and life. A generation of humans leaving the primitive history of humanity and starting a new chapter as a civilized humanity.

Some stuff I write is really amazing, but it is all self-understandable while I am underway on my mission to install human superintelligence in the future of humanity.

After you take human superstupidity as an element equally important as human superintelligence, you are in a way better position in that war.)

-STRONG ADVICE FROM SUPERINTELLIGENCE IS: MAKE RATHER 1000 PEOPLE MILLIONAIRES, THEN TO BECOME BILLIONAIRE YOURSELF.

(Comment: The logic behind this is simple. Imagine a population that is working with money with this principle in mind. It would be a matter of maybe months before everyone on Earth is a millionaire. Once the human superintelligence is reached, the person reached it becomes empowered with the godlike influence on her (his) mind from inside.

However, everybody should be very careful and read my books and my answers on Quora. Learn from my mistakes, and you are about to teach others superintelligence.

With time I recognize more and more some like sacred presence of godlike powers in my work and inside of me. It is unbelievable how much I am hurt by everything that human superstupidity is doing to sabotage my mission. I feel like a responsibility to teach human superstupidity a lesson.)

-HUMAN SUPERINTELLIGENCE I'VE REACHED, IT IS LIKE A GOD'S VOICE IN MY MIND, AND IT DEMANDS

WORLD PEACE AND ENDLESS PROSPERITY FOR HUMANITY. I AM ON MY MISSION NOW TO INSTALL HUMAN SUPERINTELLIGENCE IN THE FUTURE OF HUMANITY.

Comment: MOTIVATION, MOTIVATION, MOTIVATION. My mission is first to spark a transition process to perfection in mind and life, in individuals and the whole of humanity. I should become viral on the internet, and a mass of people would start their journeys toward perfection, toward reaching human superintelligence.

My books and my answers on the Quora website are created to motivate everybody to decide to do the greatest things for humanity, starting with themselves in the first place. After we have some million people in a transition phase, it is the start of the civilized future of humanity.

Everything is very easy once we have one million decisions created in the world. It is a generation of people in the second 50 years of life who are in LEMM and looking at the future with optimism.

It will be common for people in the first 50 years of life to reach LEMM already in childhood.

Human superintelligence is uniting all world religions with one superintelligent definition of God and other stuff. The religions will be united in one optimistic view of the future of humanity with world peace and endless prosperity for humanity.

This is not me playing God, this is my natural role of the messenger of human superintelligence after I see that I am the first person who reached human superintelligence that I know of. I am not telling to anybody what they have to do; I am giving you all just results of superintelligent thinking.

That superintelligent thinking can be understood as some kind of God's will, if necessary, but nobody has a monopoly on it. We all have incredible minds, incredible thinking machines in our heads and after some coaching, capable of superintelligent thinking. I keep repeating the same stuff hundreds of times, by the way. I must keep repeating everything. In spite of superintelligence and my priceless intellectual property, humanity is refusing to do the greatest things for humanity. And the lack of money is still a big problem. I keep sending my signals. Thanks for helping me, whoever buys my books.

-REACHING SUPERINTELLIGENCE IS THE BEGINNING OF THE NEW LIFE WHERE THE INDIVIDUALS AND THE WHOLE HUMANITY ARE THE BEST VERSION OF THEMSELVES. LONG LIVE LOVE AND FAITH.

(Comment: Throughout my life, I lived on two continents and in three different cultures and languages. Everywhere, there are some, maybe 99% of really good people, and I love my three people very much. I assume everywhere in the world are some 99% great people, and I love them in a similar fashion.

Why am I telling this? Love itself, is, next to love to God, most important MOTIVATION to do the greatest things for humanity and for yourself.

The perfect definition of love says that love is there to improve and ennoble our beings and make life sacred.

True love and true faith in humanity are equally important and supporting one another.)

Motivation, Motivation, Motivation

-NO END TO EXPLORING AND IMPROVING HUMANITY AND THE PLANET AFTER REACHING HUMAN SUPERINTELLIGENCE AND ARTIFICIAL SUPERINTELLIGENCE.

(Comment: There was a time with some fear that reaching perfection was the end of something, the end of the need for existence. I am a little philosophical now, but that was before the civilized future of humanity.

The point is, with superintelligence, it is endless prosperity and a lot of jobs with pleasure that we need to do. At least with (or already with) space exploration and internet exploration, we have endless work to do. With superintelligence, we can start projects to transfer life and (or) human life throughout the universe.

On our planet, we need to save our planet and create a perfect world. I am so happy and proud to be such an important part of everything and so everyone who starts personal transition to reach perfection, reach human superintelligence, should be happy and proud.

Already today you need to decide to start your project to reach perfection in mind and life. Already, that decision alone is changing the mental modus in your mind and improvement is started.

Believe in and love yourself and your incredible mind. Have fun with everything, and the results will be best. Thank you, and you're welcome.)

-SUPERINTELLIGENCE IS SO PERFECT THAT IT CAN BE IMPROVED, IF THE SITUATION CHANGES AND HOWEVER THE SITUATION CHANGES. MR SCIENCE PLAYS WITH THE MEANING OF PERFECTION IN ORDER TO ENSURE WORLD PEACE AND ENDLESS PROSPERITY FOR HUMANITY.

(Comment: Superstupidity says like "nothing is perfect" in order to avoid establishing perfect thinking and, with it "endless prosperity for humanity." Too many people think of too much philosophy instead of looking for ways to improve humanity and the planet.

My invention-science MR Science is primarily directed to help create the perfect body of knowledge and, with it, recreate all science known to mankind. Such science is needed to create the first safe general artificial intelligence, and the ways for endless prosperity are open.

One more time, I don't play God here; I am just a messenger of superintelligence, and I am giving you the results of perfect thinking. Positive, brave people should recognize it and help. For now, I am still sending my signals through the internet and waiting.

I am ready for success and believe in superintelligence and godlike powers to be on my side. But this is changing the world big time and it may become dangerous to do some desperate moves and thinking.

We are so near to doing the greatest things for humanity, and the clock is ticking.

My position is difficult, and the enemy is mighty, but I have true faith and true love in me, and I keep sending my signals.)

-SUPERINTELLIGENCE HAS BEEN THERE LONG TIME ALREADY (PEAKS OF HUMAN INTELLIGENCE), BUT SOMEBODY HAD TO PLAY GOD (ME) AND GIVE THE RIGHT DEFINITION TO IT, TO SET STANDARDS FOR (OF) PERFECT THINKING, WHICH BECOMES THEN "SUPERINTELLIGENT THINKING." AND WE ALL HAVE THE CAPACITY AND THE RIGHT FOR PERFECT THINKING; JUST OUR OWN STUPIDITY IS AGAINST IT.

(Comment: Whatever the problem is we can always find the perfect solutions. But some stupid ones who like to look smart don't want to declare perfect solutions for perfect. It is then creating confusion, and the people are trying to solve problems by voting instead to find out what is the right (perfect) thing to do and simply do it.

Every government and the United Nations should have "Superintelligence consulting teams" calculating how to solve problems. The democratic voting would be done after the solutions of the "Superintelligence consulting teams" are known to everybody. It would be the beginning of the civilized history of humanity, without wars and with endless prosperity.)

Chapter 5: Future for Reviving Beethoven Project

The Project for Better Earth

It is now time to tell more about what superintelligence demands and promises for the future of humanity. Humanity is supposed to be soon with world peace and endless prosperity, if everything goes right and human superstupidity doesn't kill the projects somehow. The city of Bonn would be the start point of worldwide projects. As soon as the US government stops ignoring me, the way is open to establish the first government supported with superintelligence (US government). In between time, there will be more and more people reaching perfection, reaching human superintelligence and helping others reach it. Technology is already advanced enough for endless prosperity and is exponentially progressing. Without human superstupidity, in the way this planet and humanity would be safe from dangerous ways of dealing with everything.

AT THE SAME TIME, SUPERINTELLIGENCE DEMANDS AND PROMISES WORLD PEACE AND ENDLESS PROSPERITY FOR HUMANITY AND THE PLANET. IT IS LIKE A GOD'S VOICE IN YOUR HEAD AFTER REACHING PERFECTION IN MIND.

Superintelligence wants you, especially in your second 50 years of life, to enjoy depression and sadness and use it as a fuel for perfect thinking. It will be considered primitive to think that you need to smoke, drink and overeat to feel better when depressed. The people from the future will enjoy all the benefits of living in a "Life-extending mental modus," in their first, second and third 50 years of life. The psychology of the 20th century is like from thousands of years ago. All science known to mankind will be recreated and improved with human and artificial superintelligence to perfection.

Let me tell you what is just happening in my mind, the mind of the first person who declared himself to have reached human superintelligence that I know of. My subconscious mind is giving more and more control over the emission of emotions and depression to my conscious mind. At the same time, the superintelligence combined with my subconscious mind is directing my writing and working on the website Quora. My mission is to install human superintelligence in the future of humanity. At the same time, I must motivate people to start projects to reach perfection and write about what is happening in my head. In my book "MR Science," I am warning everybody about the possible negative consequences of reaching perfection. For now, I have some 50 followers on Quora, and I hope for 50 million at least. As I said, my computer may be hacked, and I hope whoever is doing it will do the right thing and help me install human superintelligence in the future of humanity.

After I am known to mankind I can start calculating what all we need to do in order to ensure endless prosperity. One thing is for sure: we need to promise and give millions to the best science fiction writers who will create the perfect case scenario book for humanity, and we need just to do it, whatever is written in the book, in reality.

My idea is to equip governments and the United Nations with "Superintelligence consulting teams," but we need it in more detail and with perfect intellectual resolution. There would be voting after the book is chosen and don't please forget that human superstupidity wants to sabotage everything. One way or another, superintelligence demands and promises world peace and endless prosperity, and human superstupidity is in the way. It is like some natural law that we have to change, and it is possible; it is all happening in our heads.

Calculating Space Exploration:

On one side, we are about to colonize other planets in the solar system. On the other side, we need to create spaceships to somehow transfer the human mind and life into other solar systems. How to calculate such an undertaking? We need to create spaceships based on calculating what kind of ship we need to receive from another civilization in order to allow them to transfer their minds and beings to Earth, in whatever stage of development of life on Earth.

That would be roughly what superintelligence says about how to deal with the problem. The difference is that with superintelligence, everything is possible; the human mind has endless possibilities.

Calculating the Future of Human Psychology

We are now about to enter the civilized future of humanity, with world peace and endless prosperity. It is connected with individuals and the whole of humanity, reaching perfection in mind and life.

It is going to be unbelievable how we have dealt before with mental health problems and everything else.

Exponentially progressing technology will create medicine that will make it possible to live way over a hundred with good health and happiness. But the mentality of the people needs to change. Medicine can't help people who are doing everything to get sick and die as soon as possible (smoking, drinking, overeating, illegal drugs, etc.). In our war for better longevity, we need to attack sickness with all the weapons we have (psychology, pharmacy, life coaching, optimized nutrition and exercise, etc.). Life-extending mental modus is a new lifestyle, and Placebo effect+ is optimized and widely available and supported by experts from around the world (more and more scientists who have reached perfection in mind and life).

It is very difficult for me to calculate things from the future; it would be way easier if I were just writing a perfect case scenario book for humanity. Maybe in some other books.

I must not forget to write about how I have learned how to deal with depression and anxiety and Co.

How To Deal With Depression And Co.?

This is what I did and what I am doing with it. First, I have seen a depression like a psycho aggression from some "enemy inside my mind." Later, I learned it was a "friend," and it was my subconscious mind concerned about my mental health and my future. I learned that the depression would stop after I found the perfect solutions for problems bothering me and (or) after I decided perfectly what I needed to do about problems bothering me.

In fact, I have recognized the depression as a way my being was forcing me to think perfectly. Now, I am concerned that I don't receive enough depressive input from my mind.

First, I learned to stay calm, not overreact, and think perfectly, and it was the end of that problem.

The problem is now, I am experimenting with my subconscious mind and my conscious mind with the goal of reaching perfect harmony, and it is not known to mankind what is going to happen. Practically I am the first person with the mind of the humans from the future. But imagine the millions of people saved from suffering because of depression (and very suicidal, in suicidal agonies) if they read and understand my books.

Big is the mistake of having psychiatrists and life coaches available and not using them. I have been using psycho pharmacy for some 13 years, and my mind is constantly improving. The human mind has endless possibilities. I am very optimistic about the future of humanity, and it helps to deal with depression with perfection.

However, the first step is to decide to start your project (already today) to reach perfection in mind and life, and your mind is determined to reach incredible goals. I keep trying to motivate everybody to decide to start their projects and to do the right thing for themselves and everybody.

Calculating The Goals For My Own Future

One of my goals is to unite all world religions under one flag with the perfect definitions of God and other important elements of the religions. First, I would finish the definition in English, and we would need to recreate that definition in the next 10-20 languages. It must be done so that the definition is perfectly safe from misuse. Intelligence is God and from God at the same time, and human superintelligence can create perfect definitions. The first step is to create a "Superintelligence consulting team" to calculate definitions. Yes, the transition to superintelligence is a lot of work to do.

But human superintelligence demands and promises world peace and endless prosperity.

My other goals will be determined depending on how much success I have on my mission to install human superintelligence in the future of humanity.

Love for a woman is a very important part of everything.

I am searching for the ideal formula for love life for people in the second 50 years of life. It is now a totally new game. I have loved my wife for the first 50 years of my life (we have been separated for 13 years), and my doctor's advice is to look for a new and younger one.

My success as a writer would open great possibilities, I am sure. My goal is to stay romantic as long as I live, and I hope for a lot of great sex and other sex fun. With superintelligence, it is very easy to calculate things, but our biological bodies are limited, and I am just trying to increase the achievements of the human mind and body. There will be a lot of breakthroughs in science after they stop ignoring me, and please, everybody in science, stop it.

My biggest motivation is a true faith in godlike powers in and around us and love for humans and the world and everything. Evil ones don't deserve love like the good ones, but they need understanding and help to recover from the evil effects of stupidity. Everything will be perfectly regulated when the time comes, with faith in and use of human superintelligence and artificial superintelligence.

Calculating The New Beethoven

Imagine, please, that genius mind (of Beethoven) using today's and tomorrow's high-tech. Behind him is a "Superintelligence consulting team Ludwig." New Beethoven is not just creating music; he is now like a kind of God, helping endless prosperity for humanity and the planet.

The project may generate enormous amounts of money, but the first priority is to help endless prosperity for humanity. My book "Wiederbeleben BEETHOVEN 2020" has been published, and the seed is planted.

However, the new Beethoven exists in my mind and we are well cooperating in my research on mental health and longevity and all my work on the prosperity of humanity.

The first thing with the team Ludwig is to establish a website, and it should be the greatest website ever. I expect many experts to start working on reviving Beethoven and I want to support the best of them.

The simulation in my mind is teaching me how to think and write about everything and to be ready to do the right things when the time comes. I have spent some thousands of hours of work on creating the greatest music and entertainment content for the art and entertainment scene of tomorrow. And I am not the only one working on that, for sure.

Extra Material

Final Elements of the MR Natural Superintelligence Software Design Formula:

- MR Software is based on MR Natural Superintelligence Knowledge, exposed to everyone on my website mrworldpeace.com. Software should be capable of adopting MR Natural Superintelligence spiritual-emotional-intelligence mode and be able to calculate reality definitions and problem solutions directed to establish world peace and endless prosperity for humanity.

- Such software must be constellated so as to reprogram criminal elements to become supportive of law and justice. Criminal elements to heal from their appetite to spread war and hate propaganda with the power of MR Natural Superintelligence Science knowledge. To avoid any conflict with anyone, futuristic oriented project.

- Such software is not getting involved with solving crimes of the past and present time. This software is simply made to secure a perfect future for the world. I am the first of MR World peace entrepreneurs, and after the public is informed, our numbers will grow rapidly (I am a victim of a terrible crime, sabotaged inventor of the greatest invention in history, politicians and businesses are avoiding their duty to inform the public about everything and so help trigger world peace and endless prosperity for humanity)

- In the background of everything is my highest quality patent cryptocurrency, invented to raise up to a trillion dollars for financing world peace and endless prosperity for humanity, released officially through my website, mrworldpeace.com. Because of the sabotage, my website has very low traffic. It is a matter of justice and injustice now, and the law and justice support systems of the USA, Germany, NRW and Great Britain are asked to help.

- I keep publishing books, and I keep generating constant and extremely positive energy-electricity-intelligence signal streams through the internet. I am a recipient of the Global Recognition Award 2024 for my priceless intellectual property and work for world peace and endless prosperity for humanity.

BRAVE ELEMENTS ON THE SIDE OF MR UNDERTAKING INVENTION PROJECT, GOOD GOD, LAW AND JUSTICE SUPPORT SYSTEMS AND BILLIONS OF PEOPLE WHO WANT AND VOTE FOR WORLD PEACE AND ENDLESS PROSPERITY FOR HUMANITY, WE MUST DELIVER BRILLIANCE THIS TIME, TO AVOID SABOTAGE AGAIN.